To my mother and father, Zellerita and Samuel Bailey,
to my sisters, Olivia St. Louis and Aminta Duncan, and
to my partner, Theo Bleckmann

PRESTON BAILEY
CELEBRATIONS

Text by Karyn Gerhard   Photographs by John Labbe

RIZZOLI
NEW YORK

TABLE OF
CONTENTS

INTRODUCTION

Since my first book, almost ten years ago, the business of event planning has changed drastically. So, too, have the events that I am creating. No longer are they just about an abundance of flowers; they have become events on a larger-than-life scale, incorporating a myriad of elements, including architecture, set design, furniture making, lighting and art installations, and even tableware and textile design.

There are few moments in life that are truly breathtaking—those moments that are so overwhelming in their beauty, theatricality, and scope, that they transfix us with wonderment and stay with us for the rest of our lives. We of course experience them in nature—the gorgeous reds and golds of trees during the fall, the dramatic blossoms in the spring, the endless fields of wild flowers in the summer, and even the shimmering icicles and expanses of clean white snow in the winter—but rarely do they happen anywhere else. It has been my passion to create moments that evoke the same sense of awe by bringing those experiences from nature indoors.

George Bernard Shaw once said: "You see things and say, 'Why?' But I dream things that never were and say, 'Why not?'" That quote embodies how we approach every event. With the advent of new technologies in areas such as lighting and tent design, and image projection, we are no longer held to the limits of our imagination; the impossible is now possible. From a tree that encompasses an entire ballroom to twenty-foot-tall floral peacock sculptures, anything we can dream we can create.

It gives me great pleasure to share some of our most unforgettable moments in the following pages and hope that they inspire you to create your own celebrations.

DRAMATIC STATEMENTS

Regardless of the type of function, a dramatic statement is our signature element. Whether it is a cascading waterfall of flowers, a room awash in magnificent jewel tones of color, or a tree made of crystal and flowers that encompasses an entire ballroom, it is that one spectacular element that makes guests stand in wonderment. These dramatic statements are art installations on a grand, yet impermanent, scale, created for one specific moment in time; after the event they only exist in the memories of the people who experienced them.

Depending on the size of the event, a dramatic statement can be a single piece that creates excitement when a guest walks in, such as the glorious floral peacocks that flank the main staircase of a hotel. However, an event also can have a series of statements; as guests discover one, it entices them to look for others. The fashion show is an exquisite example of dramatic statements unfolding. As the guests enter, their eyes are guided upward to an enormous crystal chandelier that runs the length of a fashion-show runway. At the end of the runway appears a second statement—a set of steps enrobed in flowers to simulate a tiered cake, upon which the models enter. The lighting is also a statement, as the mood of the room completely transforms as the colors of the lights change. It is always amazing to see that the statement to which one guest responds will not necessarily be the one to which another guest responds.

Over the years, as the artistry of our dramatic statements evolved in size and scope, they have taken on the feeling of art installations. In some cases, they truly are art installations, such as the fields of light created by artist Bruce Munro for a museum event in London. This concept of the dramatic statement as an art installation is what brought me to create pieces such as the enormous floral peacocks in Covent Garden.

The goal of a dramatic statement is for a guest to take away that one element as a defining memory of an event. And when we have done that, we know we have accomplished our goal.

Opposite and following spread: For this outdoor event in Bali, the seating took center stage as the dramatic statement. Profusions of ribbons, flowers, and crystals created stunning canopies for seating areas that overlooked the ocean.

Lighting can play a very important part in an event. Here a bold statement is made with rich color, while undulating patterns of light play on the walls, bringing the room to life.

For this outdoor event, lighting designer and artist Bruce Munro was commissioned to create these fields of light for guests to move through and linger amongst. The sculptured floral balls mimic the lights to add another layer to this unique statement.

Peacocks, symbols of beauty and renewal, greet the guests as they arrive at the Hotel du Cap Eden-Roc in France. These twenty-foot-tall statues were constructed of thousands of white orchids.

This event in New Delhi included a dramatic statement that was actually hidden. The frame for this twenty-foot-tall tent was constructed entirely out of bamboo, instead of the traditional metal.

The escort arrangement—or place-card table—is the first thing a guest encounters when entering an event, and is a perfect place to make a dramatic statement. Here, cascades of ribbons, flowers, and crystals set the mood for the evening.

A twenty-five-foot-tall tree, dripping with thousands of crystals and flowers, fills an entire ballroom. This shimmering canopy is an epic realization of bringing nature indoors. Following spread: This tented bridal fashion show for the extraordinary designer Biyan featured several dramatic statements: the ceiling of thousands of crystals and flowers that spanned the entire runway, the staircase designed to look like a tiered floral wedding cake, and the runway that was also the dining table. The jewel-tone lighting created yet another statement.

These sculptured centerpieces—enormous metal trees adorned with flowers—represent another way to bring nature indoors. Following pages: In contrast to the serene blue of the dining room, intense red lighting, and modern furniture transformed a library into a sexy after-party.

THE MAGIC OF TENTS

There is something magical about an event held in a tent—a space that is built, stays up for one evening, and then disappears, only to live in people's memory. It is almost like creating a mirage.

With tents you have the best of both worlds—an event that is held outside but protected from the elements. Over the years, tent technology has improved tremendously. There are now tents of every shape and size—double-tiered tents, tents shaped as igloo-like bubbles, and so on—the options are endless. Many outdoor events also employ elaborate trailers for the bathrooms, complete with stalls and basins, which provide another place to showcase exquisite design.

Tents are perfect venues in which to create, as we are able to manipulate every element of the space. There are literally no restrictions as to what can be done. Every event must have a certain continuity—an entrance leading into an enticing foyer area and ultimately guiding guests into the big reveal of the main reception room. An event in an existing structure—a ballroom, say—is constricted by the architecture and the particular unchangeable elements of that space; a tent, on the other hand, is literally a blank canvas—a floor, four walls, and a ceiling. We are able to create the space to our exact specifications, designing the placement and style of entryways, the flow of the rooms, and even the vault of the ceiling. Instead of working around a permanent carpet or color scheme, we are able to tailor the floors, ceiling, and walls to our own interior design.

The blank canvas of a tent also provides endless decorating possibilities—covering the walls in volumes of exquisite fabric, creating a canopy ceiling dripping with ribbons and crystals, or stringing hundreds of fiber-optic cables to create a spectacular entrance. The only restrictions are the limits of our imagination.

Tents allow you to create your own world, literally anywhere in the world. They are truly the ultimate setting.

Opposite and following spread: This after-party demonstrates how important textiles are to event design. The walls of the tent and the structure over the dance floor are draped with a luxurious fringed fabric, and the ceiling is created with huge panels of woven fabric.

In this vaulted-ceiling tent, panels of mirrors line the walls and reflect the floral chandeliers hanging from the ceiling. The architectural frame of the tent is covered in fresh flowers, as are the oversize centerpieces, which are lined with garlands of jasmine.

Entrances are one of the most important elements of an event, as they move guests from one area to another while creating a gallery of surprises. Tents allow you to create your own entrance. Here, guests proceed through a series of transitional arches that lead them to the main room. Through the first arch (left) guests walk a path flanked by two sculptures of fiber optics rising from floral beds (right and following spread).

Following spread: Guests proceed through the next arch to a circular foyer tent, draped with silk and lined with oversize mirrors with floral detail. Intelligent lighting was used to change the color scheme of the room throughout the evening.

Previous spread: (left) Guests move from the first foyer tent to a light-green second foyer, showcasing a ceiling created entirely out of ribbons; (right) the bathroom trailer for the event, decorated with a vintage frame gallery. This spread: From the light-green foyer guests enter the main room of the event. New lighting technology allowed us to create a particularly spectacular dramatic statement for this room: as the guest takes a step, a flower appears on the floor, giving the illusion that as they walk, they leave a trail of flowers on the floor behind them. Following spread: (left) The traditional archways adorned with fresh flowers; (right, top) a floral sofa in the main room; (bottom) the floral centerpieces of cascading orchids adorn the tables in the dining room.

CEREMONIES

I have always loved working on ceremonies, especially wedding ceremonies, and for good reason. Weddings are a very intimate time for the couple and the family; and because they are filled with so much meaning, it is a blessing for me to share this important moment in their lives. I have been invited to create weddings all over the world; it is an amazing gift to be exposed to so many different cultures and what weddings represent for them. I revel in immersing myself in the richness of each culture and exploring ways to translate that into the design of the event. I often joke that I should be an honorary member of the United Nations!

Most cultures view weddings as a time for the ultimate celebration, bringing together family and friends that haven't seen each other for a long time. It is an opportunity to give back, to repay favors, and to honor people. Each culture has a different set of rules and protocols for the wedding ceremony and celebrates it in different ways.

Weddings can also take place in many different settings—a private home, in nature, a church, or a beautiful tent. The settings are as varied as the weddings themselves.

For the bride, her wedding is the one day in her life when the focus is absolutely on her. It is an opportunity for mothers and daughters to bond, and for the bride to start creating her own identity. Defining the style of the wedding is about pinpointing the bride's likes and dislikes. For a bride who loves winter we created a wonderland in pure white; for a wedding with an Asian influence we set the wedding in an old temple and brought in a koto player for the music.

In each of the ceremonies in this chapter you will see how tradition, culture, and a bride's personal style come together to create an event that is both exciting and memorable. And although wedding ceremonies may be different in every culture, one thing that they all have in common is that they are the ultimate entertainment.

Opposite and following spread: For this Asian-inspired ceremony held in an old temple, we created this raised platform surrounded by a moat. As the ceremony was performed on the platform, a koto player on the landing created the mood with her distinctive music.

The lush greenery in Jackson Hole, Wyoming, provided the perfect backdrop for this outdoor wedding.

For this unique church wedding, we covered the entire altar with a theatrical backdrop printed with one of the bride's favorite psalms. Another piece of inspirational text was incorporated into the runner upon which the bride walked.

The Hotel du Cap Eden-Roc in France is one of the most exquisite locations for a wedding. Here, a mirrored gazebo fringed with drapes of crystals frames the stunning hotel in the distance. Following spread: The Eden Roc does present one unique design challenge—a breathtakingly long processional aisle from the hotel to the wedding gazebo. For the wedding on the right, the aisle is flanked by large floral chandeliers; for the wedding on the left, we used chimes, which were tied down as the guests arrived, then released just before the bride walked down the aisle.

The Cotillion Room at the Pierre hotel in New York City is completely transformed into a shimmering white winter wonderland, with trees of crystals, white orchids draping the walls, and the ceiling in white silk.

Roses were the predominant décor for this outdoor wedding at the St. Regis hotel in Laguna Beach, California. The emblem at the entrance, the arches that span the processional aisle, and the gazebo were all created using thousands of these romantic flowers.

Profusions of hydrangeas and roses in fifteen-foot-tall containers soar above the processional aisle and altar for this traditional church wedding in Colombia, South America.

Floral chandeliers were created using roses, orchids, and garlands of jasmine; these flowers were repeated in the structure for the ceremony.

The muted pink and ivory flowers that adorn the chuppah were are also used in the hanging floral sculptures that draw the eye upward to the magnificent Starlight Roof at the Waldorf-Astoria hotel in New York City.

A printed floral carpet runner leads to a very clean, streamlined chuppah for this seaside wedding in Malibu, California.

Vibrant color was a very important element for this wedding in Bali. Here, a fountain of flowers greets the guests at the entrance to the event. Following spread: The color scheme followed through the rest of the ceremony, in the tall centerpieces, and in the enormous ceiling structure of cascading flowers and crystals dotted with hundreds of butterflies.

TABLE SETTINGS

At most celebrations, whether small or large, guests meet, socialize, and spend the majority of their time gathered around tables; they are the intimate places within large events.

From the moment a guest sits down, the centerpieces, china, crystal, linens, and even the chairs, all work together to create a place of comfort and beauty but also a place that constantly intrigues and entices. Guests discover ideas and themes in each element on the table. Even the serving of food is intriguing, from the way it is presented to how it works with the table setting.

The beauty of table settings is that they have the ability to work on several levels. They are the perfect stages on which to play out the theme of an event, but they are also the place for guests to eat and mingle, those theme elements becoming a functional part of the table setting. For example, as guests enter a wedding reception they are met with a sea of votive candles in hanging globes, evoking a sense of drama and romance. Those same globes then function as a canopy of intimacy once the guests are seated. By layering textures, flowers, and scents at eye level, the table becomes even more exciting.

From charming pineapple trees made from sunflowers that add a touch of whimsy, to chairs covered in an array of opulent red fabrics to evoke a sense of romance, and a setting playfully created entirely out of paper, table settings follow a concept to tell a story, create a mood, and set a tone. Tablecloths, napkins, place settings, china and stemware, centerpieces, and sculptural details (floral or otherwise), are just some of the elements we experiment with to set the scene. Even color and lighting are an effective way to tell a story, using candles shimmering in crystal votives to bathe tables in an ethereal light to give the feeling of eating under the stars. There is a great deal of flexibility when creating subtle elements of design, and the possibilities are endless.

Intimate, dramatic, romantic—anything can be conveyed with a spectacular table setting.

Opposite and following spread: The Temple of Dendur at the Metropolitan Museum of Art in New York City creates the perfect setting for any event, which is why it is one of my favorite spaces in which to work. Because of the power of the temple, the space requires centerpieces that are equally as strong and dramatic.

This very whimsical table, designed for a Williams-Sonoma event, was a great deal of fun to create. Using Williams-Sonoma products, we took a playful twist on reality, with rose-and-ribbon pies, floral shish kebabs, and sunflower pineapples.

Bringing nature indoors is one of our primary focuses, so we were thrilled when this client asked for an elegant rainforest effect for their event. Our interpretation used a profusion of green in the canopy of trees and layering of the table settings to simulate the lushness of the rain forest.

For this night of a thousand candles, guests dined under an arbor of candlelight, both indoors and outdoors. Inside, the trees were actually part of the table setting, with long floral runners atop a layer of LED lights to create a multilevel effect.

Rock 'n' roll–themed floral centerpieces adorned the tables for a rock star's birthday party.

Entertainment can be about abundance; it is a big part of any celebration. Here the beauty of abundance is interpreted by enveloping guests in opulent colors and plentiful fruits and flowers.

The centerpiece structures of cascading crystals, bathed in an ethereal blue light, were our interpretation of dining under the stars.

I have always found the use of earth tones very soothing. Here the warmth of the earth tones is enhanced by the flickering candlelight reflected in glass centerpiece sculptures and table elements, creating a sense of movement.

Here a perfect example of a table setting working on two levels. The floral arbors that rise above the tables provide a canopy of intimacy once the guests are seated. On the table are layers of rich colors and textures, completing the passionate mood for this event.

This table setting, made entirely out of paper elements—tablecloths, napkins, chair covers, and umbrella—and accented with fruits and flowers, was great fun to create. It is amazing what one can do with scissors and a glue gun.

From the explosion of ruby-red flowers to the unique chair covers, the richness of textures and layers creates surprising details in this table setting.

Individually designed chair covers can make each guest at an event feel special and unique. Here the opulent covers reflect the elements of the table design and turn each chair into a conversation piece. Following spread: (left) Dramatic lighting for an outdoor event is created with tall cornucopia-like centerpieces that also function as torches; (right) the abundant cornucopia theme is continued on the table with a multilayered runner of fresh flowers and fruits.

THE ART OF THE DETAIL

There is an old adage, "The devil is in the details," but for me, beauty is in the details. These little surprises and unexpected elements are what make creating an event a pleasure.

The success of every event depends upon the smallest components. A dramatic statement is very important, but without the details, even the grandest event can lack substance and excitement. From ribboned canopies to a charming daisy placed inside a folded napkin or the use of lush greenery for a table setting, the exquisite layering of details is what keeps guests intrigued and on a constant path of discovery throughout the event.

However, as important as details are, they needn't be extravagantly expensive. The great joy of my job is finding new, unpredictable ways to make an event come to life; recently I discovered that paper, of all things, can be one of the most versatile, colorful, and exciting elements with which to work—and it has the added benefit of being inexpensive.

Once I began to envision an entire table setting created in paper, the possibilities for its use were endless. From floral chair backs to daisy cupcake place mats of woven ribbon, paper brought an exquisite level of texture and beauty to the table while still being functional and affordable, and prompted me to look for other similarly affordable and versatile elements.

There are so many places to introduce exciting details—from the entrance, to the table, and even the chairs—the only limit is the limit of your imagination. As you will see, the details on the following pages are easily attainable, affordable, and not terribly difficult to make. Some of the techniques do require some artistry, but with a little practice and patience, creating these details can be immensely rewarding.

I hope these exquisite details will inspire you to pick up your glue gun, let your imagination run wild, and use every element at your disposal to create details that make your event truly memorable.

Opposite and following two spreads: This whimsical table is created with yarn, felt, and paper. The wonderful felt overlay strips on the table are also woven into chair covers adorned with roses made of felt. The low centerpieces showcase apricot-colored paper peonies placed in yarn-covered containers. Even the decorative giveaways are covered in felt, yarn, and buttons.

Classic accordion-paper wedding bells were the inspiration for the theme of this wedding table. The topiary centerpiece is made up of these bells, with beautiful green chrysanthemums and gerbera daisies at the base to bring a splash of color. The chair covers are accented with folded paper flowers, and the place settings use soft LED votive lights and individual daisy cupcakes as statements.

Ribbons and paper in jewel tones are used as the basis for this colorful table. Pink paper peonies sit in ribbon-covered canisters, while a canopy of flowers made entirely of ribbons hangs overhead. Woven ribbon is used to create the place mats and runners; the ribbon theme is continued in the chair backs, each woven in a different design.

This lush table setting is reminiscent of the rainforest in my native Panama. The setting is made entirely from leaves and moss: for the centerpiece, the pedestal is covered with woven striped leaves and topped with large monsteria leaves for a dramatic statement, with moss and folded monsteria leaves for the base. Leaves are used as napkin holders, and fabric with a leaf texture brings the entire table together.

TRANSFORMATIONS

Transformation. This is the essence of what we do, and where our business has been headed since we first began planning events. The clients who come to us are looking for an event that is out of the ordinary—they ask us to transform a space into something so unique and wonderful that it can never again be replicated. From America to the South of France, Indonesia, and the Middle East, I have had the pleasure of working with clients who have faith in my vision, and the luxury of giving me the freedom to do something truly extraordinary.

Every event I do means so much to me, and takes me on its own path of discovery. Those paths have all led me to this point. The creative vision, the complete transformation of a space, the grandeur and spectacle—the events in this chapter are some of the most comprehensive and larger-than-life events of my career to date. They not only represent what can be achieved, but also my absolute joy in working in this creative, challenging, and ever-expanding industry. These events inspire me to explore new paths of creativity, and I am excited about the possibilities to come. For me, this journey has only begun.

This wedding in the Waldorf-Astoria hotel was for the son of one of our most sophisticated clients, a Brazilian woman of impeccable taste who is well known for hosting spectacular celebrations. The wedding was split into two parts: an elegant ceremony, held in the spectacular Starlight Roof room, and a festive reception, held in the Grand Ballroom. As the client comes from a culture that understands what celebration is all about, this was a wonderful challenge.

The client had always loved the stained-glass windows in churches and synagogues and wanted to use that as the theme for the ceremony. This gave us an opportunity to incorporate the magnificent Art Deco skylight (from which the room gets its name) in a very synchronistic manner. The theme played out in several ways: from a series of stained-glass trees, created from hand-painted Plexiglas, which flanked the main aisle leading to the chuppah, to a Tiffany-style landscape printed on fabric that was stretched across the wall of the chuppah and lit from underneath.

The atmosphere for the reception in the Grand Ballroom was one of playful sophistication. Enormous circles of hanging crystals, each with its own mirrored ball, created a mirage of sparkling light; the centerpieces were profusions of flowers atop bases sculpted from hundreds of roses and miniature hybrid chrysanthemums. To make the room cohesive we created a dance floor on printed vinyl and laid it over the existing carpet. It was a perfect setting for guests to party all night.

WALDORF-ASTORIA WEDDING
New York, NY

Les Jardins
de Guerny
10

For this tented event, a young, fun, and energetic client requested a sit-down-dinner that would also act as a theater for a series of performances throughout the evening. It was necessary to create an environment that was exciting and dynamic, and the beauty of working with this client was that she was open to all possibilities.

Every detail was very important to the client, from the entrance floor with a runner of Balinese textile under Plexiglas, to the dramatic proscenium entrance with her monogram against a backdrop of thousands of roses. The stage was a replica of the Hollywood Bowl, made entirely of crystals and illuminated in an array of colors that changed throughout the evening. The table settings were layered with surprises, from the tablecloths and chair covers adorned with explosions of festive ribbons, to the raised glass placemat set atop beautifully designed flowers, and the personalized, custom-made chinaware. In order to make sure every seat had good visibility of the stage, the tables that lined the room had canopies of ribbons, flowers, and crystals, while the tables in the middle were adorned with low floral centerpieces.

For the after-party we created a night club in an adjacent tent. Once inside, guests were greeted with several large-scale chandeliers, sculpted out of drinking glasses and illuminated with rods of nightclub light, which were suspended from a fabric checkerboard ceiling. For another level of fun, a dance pole was set into the main chandelier. A spectacular light show made the after-party truly extraordinary.

TENT RECEPTION
Bali

Reinventing existing spaces is always exciting, and this birthday celebration was no exception. Our client wanted to create a night club for his wife. Gotham Hall in New York City is a perfect setting for any function, but for this particular event—an intimate birthday celebration for 125 people with a black-and-white theme—the enormous ballroom posed certain challenges as well as some unique possibilities.

Working with the fantastic Vivia Costalas, the first challenge was coping with the imposing, turn-of-the-century architecture. In order to create a sense of intimacy, we created a truss system over the space and draped the room in volumes of sheer fabric, leaving the center exposed so that guests could view the 3,000-square-foot stained-glass skylight. Raised banquettes lined the room, creating a nightclub environment and enhancing the atmosphere of intimacy.

The second challenge in transforming the room was creating a dynamic, exciting event using only black and white. Black-beaded lampshades and stark-white linen napkins stitched with the honoree's initial, and intricately patterned chair covers were all custom-made for the event; white roses set in silver footed tureens completed the table settings. Using silver in the place setting and as accents on the table not only added another dimension, but its reflective quality made the tables shimmer in the candlelight. Even the birthday cake incorporated elements of the theme in a playful way, and a hand-painted vinyl floor with the honoree's name pulled the entire event together. But the real dramatic statement of the event was the mirrored proscenium encompassing the stage, upon which Tony Bennett performed.

The environment we created was so comfortable, warm, and welcoming, that many guests wanted to stay all night—which is always the mark of a truly spectacular celebration.

BIRTHDAY CELEBRATION
Gotham Hall, New York

This birthday party, for one of New York City's most noted male personalities, took place in December at the Allen Room at Jazz at Lincoln Center. Instead of creating a performance space within another event, here we had an empty theater that needed to be transformed into a festive lounge and performance space. This event was a lot of fun to create, as the client wanted a whimsical, almost tongue-in-cheek theme. The concept for the event came from the painting of a cake blazing with candles, entitled *Old Age*, by artist Matt Zumbo. As the guests walked into the cocktail area, panels emblazoned with the image surrounded the room, giving the event a sense of sophisticated playfulness. At the center of the room we created a custom-made bar with thousands of stacked glasses, giving the illusion of a tiered glass cake.

The guests entered the performance space through two etched Plexiglas sculptures, at the center of which read "50 is the new 40." As guests walked into the theater, with its floor-to-ceiling windows that overlook Central Park, they were met with hanging ten-foot spheres covered with thousands of LED candles, which continued the festive theme. (These spheres could also be seen from the street, and worked as a fun contrast to the holiday decorations on the floor below.) All of the theater seating had been removed and lounge furniture put in its place, which created a comfortable, intimate atmosphere in which to enjoy the buffet dinner and musical performances.

JAZZ BIRTHDAY
AOL Time Warner Center, New York City

This event presented possibly the most challenging transformation of my career—turning a large, empty convention center into a venue for a royal wedding. The raw space meant that we did not have to contend with any existing architectural elements, but it also had no focal point or flow. For this event I had the privilege of working with floral master Daniel Ost to execute the theme of lush greenery and nature.

First, we created an entrance area that also served to set the tone for the entire event. Guests entered through a floral gallery of white walls with vases of flowers placed on clear shelves of varying heights.

The most essential element for the large space was to create a centralized foundation or anchor for the main room. For this we erected an enormous proscenium made of hundreds of thousands of flowers which floated over a Plexiglas base; the spray from fountains set behind gave the base a cool, frosted look. A long, lighted walkway led to a leaf-inspired gold chaise, designed and created specifically for this event, where the princess sat to receive her guests.

To continue the theme of vibrant greenery, hundreds of clear containers filled with water and rimmed with flowers were suspended from the ceiling. The walls were draped fabric upon which images of trees had been silk-screened; standing in front of the panels were Plexiglas tree trunks with a profusion of floral foliage.

Fountains with water cascading over etched pylons broke up the large space and completed the lush, soothing atmosphere.

ROYAL WEDDING
Abu Dhabi

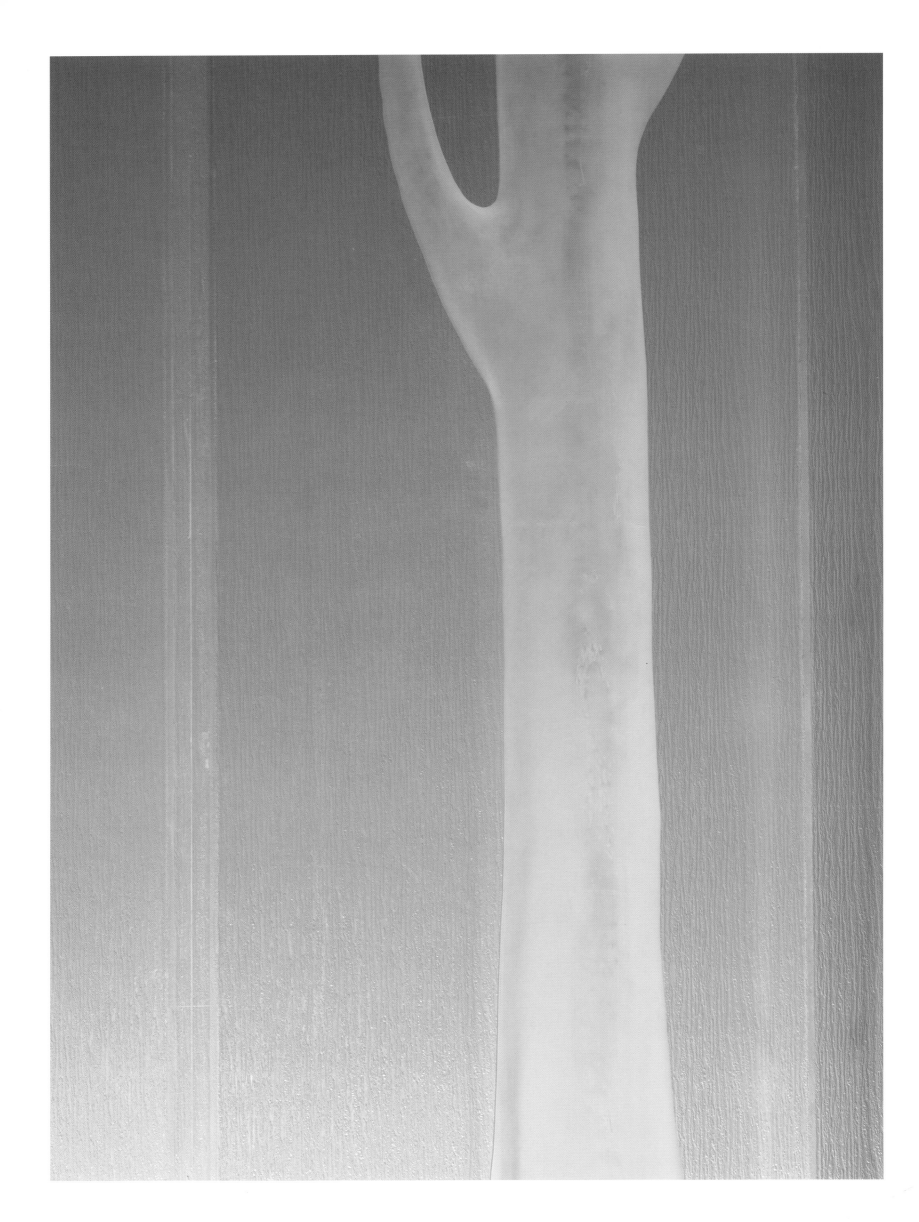

The client for this party is extremely sophisticated and very specific about how she wanted the event to look. It was important to her for the space to be open and inviting, layered with interesting details, but with very clean lines and an uncluttered look.

The event was divided into two sections—cocktails and dinner. For the cocktail area we decided to use a round tent with a see-through roof, so that the night sky became the ceiling, allowing for a fantastic view of the fireworks later on. In the center of the tent we created a twenty-foot-square floor chandelier, made entirely out of flowers and crystals, which cascaded into an ice sculpture. The flowers encased in ice acted as an anchor for the oversize chandelier. The bar and buffet surrounded the sculpture, and printed scrims with trellises of fresh flowers enhanced the color theme.

It was important to continue the theme of sophisticated simplicity in the dining room. The tent was such a beautiful structure that we did not need to drape the ceiling; the only adornment was a series of crystal and halogen chandeliers by lighting artist Bruce Munroe. The beautifully simple table settings of clear dinnerware and beeswax candles designed for the event were offset by the single bold statement of the floral centerpiece. To complete this magnificent exercise in understated elegance, a hand-painted dance floor was installed, which reflected the warm glow of the halogen lights and acted as the anchor for the room.

WEST COAST PARTY

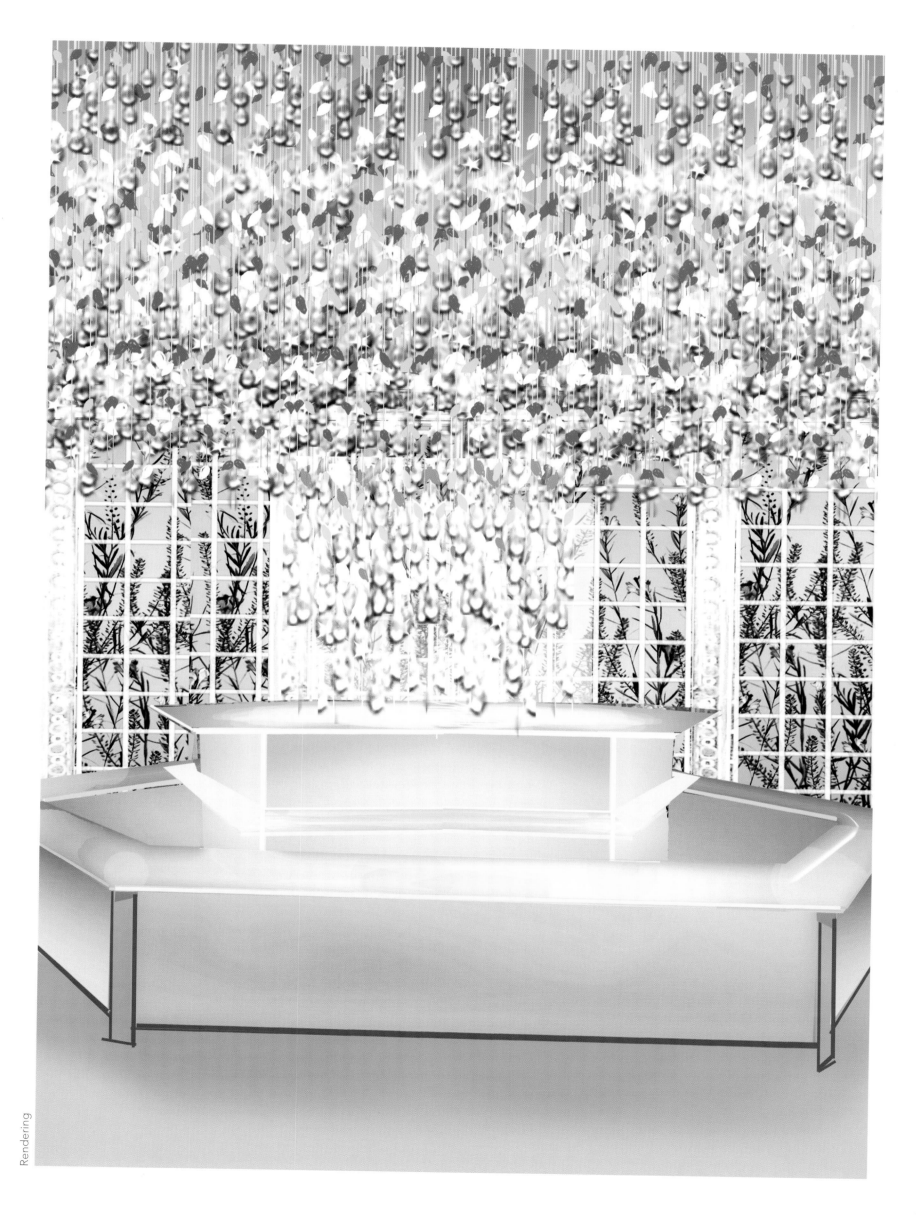

I had the pleasure and privilege of creating a wedding for the beautiful Jennifer Lustig, one of the daughters of the most visionary client I have ever worked with, Mrs. Debbie Lustig and her supportive and loving husband Mr. James Lustig. Mrs. Lustig's brilliance for hosting events comes from her experience of entertaining with such grace, generosity, and attention to detail.

Even though the Century Plaza Hotel is a beautiful space, it was important to adapt it to the sensitivity of Mrs. Lustig. In the ceremony room, the bride walked down an aisle lined with trees of cascading blossoms to a chuppah crowned with layers of Swarovski crystals and twined with orchids and roses. The walls of the room were draped with soft fabrics to complete the elegant, classic look.

For the cocktail area we created a sophisticated garden, outlining the walls with hedges and setting a round bar lined with mirrors and hedges in the center of the room. One of the most delicate elements of the cocktail party was the explosions of orchids set in vases sculpted of ice.

Mrs. Lustig had the brilliant concept of using swans as a motif for the reception. I was thrilled, as I love creating floral sculptures; they are the most artistic of endeavors and one of my favorite aspects of any event. The bridal dais was an oversize table with a beautiful Sylvia Weinstock cake flanked by two swans. In order to keep the room working on different levels, some of the tables were adorned with swans while others had umbrellas of raining crystals or profusions of flowers. The dance area was treated as a huge living room, with comfortable seating surrounding the hand-painted floor.

I had the pleasure of being a guest at this wedding. Because of Mrs. Lustig's savvy in entertaining, the guests never wanted to leave, and the party continued into the wee hours of the morning.

CALIFORNIA WEDDING
Century Plaza Hotel, Los Angeles

Author John O'Donohue once wrote, "When a destination becomes gracious, the journey becomes an adventure of beauty." These words embody the work that we do. Since the very beginning we have been on an odyssey of creating beauty and magic, exploring new techniques, meeting exciting challenges, and pushing boundaries. Each event is a step on our road of discovery, and the success is reflected in our productions and client relationships. Our goal is to give our clients that one unforgettable day; of course, we may not always get it perfect, but most of the time we come very close.

This desert dreamscape was a challenge in every sense of the word, but a challenge that we relished. The perfect combination of new technologies, theatrical elements, and dramatic statements utilized for this event allowed us to use our imagination in new and exciting ways.

Like a mirage, this entrancing "city" appeared and disappeared in the desert for just one day. The entire event was encased in a dome equivalent to a football field in size, and accommodated seating for 1500 guests plus 500 service people. Inside the dome we created a myriad of changing environments using innovative lighting technology; with the push of a button a starry night sky covered the interior of the dome and changed patterns throughout the evening.

At the entrance, several moats of floating flowers greeted the guests and led them to a spectacular sunken dance floor and a trompe l'oeil stage beyond. For the dance floor, we laid down a mosaic of flowers and lights and covered it with Plexiglas to give a sense of depth. The dramatic statement—an umbrella of flowers hung over a seating area—provided a visual break in the dome, as well as secluded space for conversation. The jewel tones used throughout made this mirage truly exquisite.

Although this extraordinary event was one of the most exciting transformations to date, it is by no means the end of our adventure of beauty. This is a growing industry, and we are still discovering new technologies, exploring the unknown, and growing. We have not yet reached the limits of our imagination, nor the destination of our journey.

DESERT DREAMSCAPE

ABOUT PRESTON

For nearly thirty years, Preston Bailey has tested the limits and expanded the possibilities of event design. Often referred to as "art installations," Preston's work transforms raw, ordinary spaces into sumptuous theatrical environments, translating his clients' fantasies to awe-inspiring reality.

Born and raised in the verdant, tropical paradise of Panama, Preston Bailey left for New York in 1969, and has lived there ever since.

Preston has earned a reputation as the world's preeminent event designer. His signature style combines elements of architecture and set design with exuberant and harmonious color palettes, sensuous textures, shapes that are both structured and organic, and modern adaptations of traditional settings to excite the senses in profound ways. Inspired by the beauty of the natural world, Preston is known for taking small, simple elements and changing, reshaping, and repeating them in many layers to create spectacular dramatic statements. Preston has created one-of-a-kind events, including the most extravagant weddings and galas, for celebrities and royal families across the globe. His work has attracted such clients as Donald Trump, Oprah Winfrey, Uma Thurman, Donna Karan, Liza Minnelli, Matt Lauer, Catherine Zeta-Jones and Michael Douglas, Laurence Fishburne, Emmett Smith, and Bill Cosby.

Preston has written three bestselling books: *Design for Entertaining*, *Fantasy Weddings*, and *Inspirations*. In addition to his many public speaking engagements, he was also the host of *Preston Bailey, Mr. Fabulous* which aired on the Oh! Oxygen network—the network's highest-rated program to date. Preston's numerous television appearances include *Oprah*, *Martha Stewart*, *Entertainment Tonight*, *Access Hollywood*, *Extra*, *CBS Early Show*, and *Today*. Preston has also been featured in national and international publications such as *Vogue*, *Town & Country*, *Elle Décor*, *Harpers Bazaar*, *InStyle*, *Martha Stewart*, *The New York Times*, *The New York Post*, *The New York Daily News*, *People*, *Us Weekly*, and *Hello!*.

ACKNOWLEDGMENTS

John Lennon once said, "A dream you dream alone is only a dream. A dream you dream together is reality." Turning the dreams of these events into reality is a truly collaborative effort, as was the creation of this book. I could not have done either without this group of generous, dedicated, and talented people.

First and foremost, my deepest love and thanks go to my partner and companion in life's journey, Theo Bleckmann.

In making the dream of this book a reality, I had the pleasure of working with an absolutely fantastic team. My gratitude goes to Jill Cohen, for her talent and genius in the book industry; to my photographer, John Labbe, for his patience, his artistic eye, and for always getting the perfect shot; to our designer, Sam Shahid, for his beautiful, thoughtful decisions—seldom am I able to work with such a true visionary; to my editor, Kathleen Jayes, for her graciousness and perseverance in putting the book together; to my writer, Karyn Gerhard, for her ability to create magic with words; and to publisher Charles Miers, for believing in this project and giving us the space to expand.

I am blessed with great friends who have also been part of this journey. My love and thanks go to: my longtime friend and mentor, Vincente Wolf for his wisdom; to my confidante, Marcy Blum, for her love and giving heart; to Erwin Gonzalez, for his support and humor; to Peter Azrak, for his guidance; and to Linda Stern, Sandy Keidan, Daniel Delburg, and Sylvia Weinstock, for their love and support.

Running this business takes the tireless efforts of a dream crew. Working with them is an absolute joy. My unending appreciation and thanks go to: Sean Low, for his ability to see ahead; to Anne Crenshaw, for her financial vision; to Michael Speir for his keen design eye; to Jee Young Sim, for her true originality; to Matthew Myhrum, for his fantastic technical design; to Sanaw Ledrod, a true floral genius; to Nadine Jervis, for understanding my vision; to Dominga Gardner, for

her inspired public relations work; to Luis Fernando, for his loyalty and caring; to Eduardo, Pedro, Junior, Kate, and Robin, who are all truly amazing; to Iqbal Hayder, the world's greatest floral manager; to Oscar Simeon Jr., for his talent and genuine grace; to Rae Simpson, my personal assistant, who always keeps me on the right path; and Donna and David from Summit Productions, for their keen understanding of the world market. Last but not least, my deepest appreciation goes to Vivia Costalas, the manager of my business, for her dedication, attention to detail, and positive energy.

I would like to give a very special thanks to my partners in Jakarta: Mrs. Meity for her vision; Karen Kwek for her Public Relations genius; the amazing designer Mrs. Dian; and Tania, Dani, and Didi. To my partners in India, I'd like to thank: Mr. Vikas Gutgutia for being an amazing visionary; Mrs. Meeta Gutgutia; and Mr. Pawan Gadia for his business guidance. To my partner in Bahrain, Shaheera Abdul, thank you.

A business like this does not exist without clients, and it has been my privilege to work with some truly extraordinary, visionary people. My gratitude goes to: The Royal Family of Abu Dhabi, Durrat Al Bahrain, The Al Mutawa family, Lauren Amos and Tyler Clayton, Mr. and Mrs. Annisomova, Adinda Bakrie and Seng Hoo Ong, Erica Baxter and James Packer, Mr. Donny Deutsch, Mr. and Mrs. Dorros, Janessa Dyer and Mark Bailey, Mr. and Mrs. Farouki, The First Family of Gabon, Gail Golden and Carl Icahn, Mr. and Mrs. Goodfriend, Mrs. Natalia Gottret and Mr. Sebastian Echavarria, Mr. and Mrs. Lustig, Arndt Oesterle and Mimma Cardone at A&O Management, The Royal Family of Qatar, Nikki Reinhardt, Mr. and Mrs. Riggio, Mr. and Mrs. Chella Safra, Mr. and Mrs. Saperstein, United Technologies, and Linda Vester and Glenn Greenberg.

The journey of my life and career has been one of discovery, perseverance, and consciousness. Working with all of these people

has made the path smoother, and the experience a joyous one. I look forward to many more years of discovering paths and turning dreams into realities with these extraordinary people.

Isaac Newton once said, "If I have seen further than others, it is by standing on the shoulders of giants." In making these dream events reality I have had the honor to work with giants from all over the world. My deepest appreciation goes to the following:

BAHARAN: Alia Flowers, Tariq Al Khaja at Yousif Qassim Art Center, Banyan Desert Spa & Resort, Lawrence Rodricks at Showtech Productions WLL

COLUMBIA: Maria Elena Baena, William Baena, Catherdral Santa Catalina De Alehandria, Jaun Del Mar, Stella Feo, Nina Garcia, Giovanni Lanzoni, Simone Lejour, Fernando Munoz, Museo Naval, Carmen Otero, Senora Mariella Para de Echevarria, German Poledo, Cristina Uricochea, Santa Clara Hotel, Santa Teresa Hotel

FRANCE: Kim Bendack, CMX Event Production, Deco Flamme, Grand Hotel du Cap-Eden Roc, Jean-Michele Louis at ECA2, Lisa Vorce

INDIA: Ashish Boobna, Mona Rajsheree Boobna, Ferns N' Petals, Bipin Gupta, Saheb Satnam Singh Kohli, Lalita Raghav

INDONESIA: Farez Al Junied, Anansa Flower Garden, Toto Artho and Budi Hernowo at Rekacitra, Biyan, Mas Boy, The Dharmawangsa Hotel, Rubiana Fajar, Saverina Fajar, Fares, Flora Linens, Floral Supplies, Gusri, I-Leimena, Sylvain Julien and Olivier Piganiol and The Dharmawangsa Hotel: The Nirwana Resort and Spa at Le Meridian, Poppy, PT Bina Floral Lestari, Quality Technical, Benny Raj, Rizal, Jenny Wiano at Anansa Flower Garden, Eka D. Widiyanto at Stupa Caspea

KUWAIT: Faisal Amir at Productions Co., Noor Al Mutawa for flowers, Nuef Al Mutawa for confectionery

UAE: Krikor Astorian at Al Khayalee, Saif Al Ghandi and Akran Juna at WUD Flowers, Carole Nohra

UNITED KINGDOM: Beverly Churchill at Covent Garden London, Ghislaine Kohler, Al Laycock at Jackie Cooper Public Relations, Living Props Ltd., Bruce Munro Ltd.

UNITED STATES: A & R Sewing Co., Accent Décor, Inc., Frank Alexander, Arts Pavillion, Baked it Myself, Bazar Fabrics, Inc., Beta Iron Works Inc, Better Mousetrap, The Century Plaza Hotel, Cipriani, Classic Party Rentals, Clear Memories, Cloth Connection, The Cube Lady, Dutch Flower Line, Inc, Fabric Resources International Ltd., Fabricut, Fellowship Bible Church of NWA, Fischer & Page Ltd., Jill Fortney, Frost Lighting, G. Page Wholesale Flowers, Inc., Gotham Hall, Hi-Tech Events, Igmor Crystal Lite Corp., J. Van Vliet New York, Jazz at Lincoln Center, Karl's Event Rentals, Lasting Art, Paula Le Duc, Levy Lighting, Inc., Liba Fabrics Corp, The Mandarin Hotel, Mayesh Wholesale Flowers, The Metropolitan Museum of Art, The Nimitz Conference Center, Nuage Designs, Inc., Okamoto Studio, Inc., Olivier Chang Catering & Events, Party Rental Ltd., Piedmont Travel, Planter Resource, Inc., St. Regis Hotel – Laguna Beach, St. Regis Hotel – NY, Shadow Valley Country Club, Showman Fabricators, Something Different Party Rentals, Pat Strananhan, Starlight Orchestra and Productions, Task Delivery Event, Treasure Island, US Evergreens, Inc. , Mindy Weiss, The Waldorf-Astoria Hotel, Wildflower Linen, Williams-Sonoma, Yale Design, Zolico Linens

Marie Lynn Wagner
Designer

Ann Crenshaw
Controller

Eduardo Martins
Associate Operations
Manager

Michael Speir
Creative Director

Robin Scott
Administrator

John Labbe
Photographer

Dominga Gardner
Public Relations Director

Matthew Myhrum
Production Designer

Jee Young Sim
Designer/Stylist

Vivia Costalas
Executive Director
of Preston Bailey
Entertainment and
Set Designs

Sean Lowe
President

Thomas Baker
Designer

Brian Kelly
Designer

Luiz Fernando Leite
Executive Operations
Manager & Estimator

Suwat Laorawat
Florist

Olivia St. Louis
Administrator

Yessid Ortiz
Florist

Iqbal Hayder
Director of
Floral Production

Rae Simpson
Administrator
and Assistant
to Preston Bailey

Marjeth Cummings
Florist

Deborah Bloom
Florist

Samron Panpinyo
Florist

Oscar Siemeon Jr.
Assistant
Floral Manager

Carlos Belo Jr.
Director of
Transportation

Pedro Santos
Production Assistant

Angkhana
Chermsirivatana
Florist

Sanaw Ledrod
Director of
Floral Design

Kesanee Ortiz
Florist

First published in the United States of America in 2009
by Rizzoli International Publications, Inc.
300 Park Avenue South
New York, NY 10010
www.rizzoliusa.com

DESIGN BY SAM SHAHID

Distributed in the U.S. trade by Random House, New York
2009 2010 2011 2012 / 10 9 8 7 6 5 4 3 2 1

Printed in China

ISBN-13: 978-0-8478-3194-4
Library of Congress Catalog Control Number: 2008939339